DO YOU WANT CAKE OR CRUMBS IN YOUR MARRIAGE?

DR. MYESHI WILLIAMS-BRILEY

DO YOU WANT CAKE OR CRUMBS IN YOUR MARRIAGE?

Copyright © 2019– All Rights Reserved Dr. Myeshi Briley

This book is copyright protected and is intended for personal use only. No parts of this publication may be reproduced in any form or by any means, including printing, scanning, photocopying, or otherwise unless explicitly stated. Any attempts to amend, sell, distribute, paraphrase, or quote the contents of this book, without the consent of the author or copyright owner can and will result in legal action.

Please note that the details included within this book are for informational purposes only. The publisher and author have made every effort to ensure the accuracy of the information contained within this book. However, they make no warranties as to the completeness of the contents herein, and hence hereby declaim any liability for errors, omissions, or contrary interpretation of the subject matter.

ISBN Number# 978-1-7346196-0-7
ESHI CO Publishing

Disclaimer

The information contained cannot be considered a substitute for treatment as prescribed by a therapist or other professional. By reading this book, you are assuming all risks associated with using the advice, data, and suggestions given below, with a full understanding that you, solely, are responsible for anything that may occur as a result of putting this information into action in any way – regardless of your interpretation of the advice.

DEDICATION

Dedication to God that has watched me weather many storms and come out greater than I ever entered. To all the strong women, and men I have meet over the years in my life. My team that works with me daily, my mentors and my very close circle of friends. You have to love a journey to understand a journey. I also dedicate my book to the universe.

ACKNOWLEDGMENT

Deuteronomy 1:11 (The LORD God of your fathers make you a thousand times so many more as ye are, and bless you, as he hath promised you!)

1:12 How can I myself alone bear your cumbrance, and your burden, and your strife?

1:13 Take you wise men, and understanding, and known among your tribes, and I will make them rulers over you.

1:14 And ye answered me, and said, The thing which thou hast spoken is good for us to do.

CONTENTS

Introduction	1
Chapter 1 Defining Emotional Affairs: Are They Real	5
Chapter 2 The Impact of Emotional Affairs: How Does It Make You Feel	14
Chapter 3 How Strong Is An Emotional Affair	25
Chapter 4 Is My Marriage Repairable? And Do I Even Want To Repair It?	35
Chapter 5 Can A Marriage Survive An Emotional Affair?	43
Chapter 6 What Can I Do To Heal Myself For The Future?	55
Chapter 7 Healing Your Marriage	64
Conculsion	74
About The Author	77

DR. MYESHI WILLIAMS-BRILEY

INTRODUCTION

Let's begin this book by asking ourselves this very critical question: "Who gets married to say they want a divorce?" Let me answer that for you: NO ONE DOES. When someone loves you, they see something that's worth something in you. Even couples who go into a marriage with prenuptial agreements signed have only signed these prenups to protect themselves in the case of eventualities. They still hope for the very best in their marriages.

So Why Do Marriages Pack Up?

Why do marriages die? The answer to these questions is very easy. Marriage dies when you stop trying and that's on both parts; men and women.

I have seen many marriages fail because one or both partners failed to follow the Biblical injunction in John 15:12 which says, "My command is this: Love each other as I have loved you." We are no longer loving each other wholeheartedly and putting the needs of our partners ahead of ours. Today, there are three sides in a marriage, which are "the truth", "the husband's side" and "the wife's side". It need not be.

DO YOU WANT CAKE OR CRUMBS IN YOUR MARRIAGE?

If you want to work on your marriage, this book is for you. You may have cheated on your partner emotionally or you may have been the one who was cheated on; as long as you are both willing to move past the past and build a new future together, this book is for you.

Or perhaps, none of you has cheated on the other (yet) but you feel a disconnect between you and want to salvage your marriage. If you are in this kind of situation, this book will also help you.

But before we go forward, ask yourself this question; "Do you want cakes or crumbs in your marriage?"

If you want the cake, you have to work on it because nothing good comes easy, and if you want something better than good, you have to put in extra effort. But it is doable, and the beauty of a marriage that has been worked on is brilliant.

In this book, I will charge you to understand that marriage is not the place to stand up for your rights. According to 1 Corinthians 7:3-4, "The marriage bed must be a place of mutuality—the husband seeking to satisfy his wife, the wife seeking to please the husband." Marriage is a decision to serve the other, whether in bed or in everyday life. If you get this single fact and get it right, you have won half the battle.

I hope to see you on the other end of this book with a stronger marriage. For those whose trust has already been broken, I pray you find the healing and the courage to work things through.

DR. MYESHI WILLIAMS-BRILEY

I am praying that you choose the cake, rather than the crumbs.

And I hope and pray that you enjoy your very own version of happily ever after, starting today.

DO YOU WANT CAKE OR CRUMBS IN YOUR MARRIAGE?

NOTES

CHAPTER 1
DEFINING EMOTIONAL AFFAIRS: ARE THEY REAL?

An emotional affair occurs when someone who is already in a committed relationship invests emotional energy and time with and into another person outside of the primary (mostly marital) relationship. The person not only devotes more of their emotional energy outside of their marriage but also receives emotional companionship and support from the new relationship. When conducting an emotional affair, an individual feel closer to the other person and may experience swelling sexual chemistry or tension towards this person.

Most emotional affairs start innocently enough as friendships, but the platonic friendship begin to form a strong emotional bond as time goes on, and this strong emotional bond hurts the intimacy of the spousal relationship. A human being's emotional energy is limited, and when a spouse is sharing intimate thoughts and feelings with someone else, an emotional affair has developed.

When emotional affairs first start, most people view it as harmless. There is usually no intent for these friendship bonds to become anything more. Despite the original intent, the line between close friendships and emotional affairs is thin, and it is important to understand that emotional affairs can also quickly lead to flirtation and sexual encounters. In fact, emotional affairs are often gateway affairs leading to full-blown sexual infidelity. Statistically, about half of emotional involvements do eventually turn into full-blown affairs, sex and all.

Emotional affairs can wreak havoc on the marriage as well as the family. We only have a certain amount of emotional energy and when we are not focusing this energy on our spouse, there is a need to find out where this might be directed at.

Although cheaters are often technically guilt free in an emotional affair because no sex is involved, their partners often view the emotional affair as harmful as a sexual affair.

For some individuals, the most painful and hurtful consequence of an emotional affair is the sense of deceit, betrayal and lies. Any part of your life that is kept essentially a secret from a spouse is dangerous to the trust between partners.

The definition of emotional affairs as stated above thus shows that emotional affairs are very real. It is a phenomenon that is in our world to stay, and it is a phenomenon that has shattered many previously solid relationships.

How An Emotional Affair Differs From A Platonic Friendship

A major factor that differentiates a friendship from an emotional affair is the secrecy. Many people will at this point sigh a sigh of relief and believe that they are off the hook, but just before you do, let's examine this issue a little bit further. Yes, it is possible that your partner knows of the friendship and the times spent together, but if you are keeping certain conversations or details a secret, there is a serious problem.

Let's go even further. What would your spouse think if they were to sit at another table and watch the two of you, or if they were to overhear your conversation? Would you have a problem having him or her witness your mannerisms, the way you touch each other, and the tone of your voice? If you will have a problem with this, there is a problem.

The next aspects of emotional affairs are daydreaming or fantasizing. If you are daydreaming about spending even more time with your friend, there is a problem. And this brings us to the next one; alone time. Are you purposely and actively creating reasons for you and this special friend to be alone, and do you find yourself feeling that other friends or your partner are getting in the way of your time alone with your friend? Yes, you might not be having sex, and may not even be thinking in that direction yet, but if spending time alone with your friend is becoming a priority for you ahead of all other things, you are courting trouble.

While there is nothing wrong with being there for a friend in good and or bad times, if this friend of yours is becoming your primary source of emotional companionship and support; there is a problem because this is the role that we as spouses should be filling for one another.

Another thing that differentiates a friendship from an emotional affair is the sexual attraction or chemistry. We definitely will meet people that we are attracted to in our lives, and that of itself is not a problem. If you are, however, sexually attracted to your special friend and you remain friends while trying to ignore it, you are playing with fire. This just makes it worse and much more intense.

When you put all, or some of these together, please know that this friendship is not exactly what you think it is, but something deeper. You are in very dangerous territory and while you may not have crossed the line yet, odds are that you will.

It is so very easy for a platonic friendship to grow into an emotional affair because all it takes is lots of time, emotional investment and just a little denial, and this is why it is important for spouses to have very clearly defined boundaries when it comes to friendships and stick to these and respect them. It is important to talk about these boundaries with your spouse often and really be honest with yourself when doing a little introspection regarding friendships in your life.

A platonic friendship can grow into an emotional affair when the investment of personal and intimate information crosses the limit set by the married couple. You should understand that an emotional affair is cracking open a door that needs to remain closed.

How Common Are Emotional Affairs And Why Do They Happen

Emotional affairs are increasingly common. According to a study, around 45 percent of men and 35 percent of women have admitted to having some sort of emotional affair, which is more than 20 percent more than people who admit to having a physical affair.

Another research involving 90,000 men and women found that 78.6 percent of men and 91.6 percent of women admitted to having an emotional affair. The thing is that, most people have committed emotional infidelity at some point—an affair of the heart, without physically cheating on a significant other—and women may cheat more than men in this way. One reason why women are more likely to have emotional affairs is parallel to the reason men tend more to cheat physically. While men tend to have more physical needs, women have more emotional ones.

One reason for the commonality in emotional affairs is that many people don't view emotional cheating as cheating at all. People can certainly have close friendships with people of the opposite sex, but having an emotional affair goes further than friendship, and the problem is that not everyone knows when they have crossed that line. It is so easy to connect with a new person on social media or through a text, and this now makes emotional affairs easier to start and easier to hide.

Another reason for emotional affairs is that people are so busy these days and don't take the time to connect emotionally with their spouses. Because of this, they may not view these spouses as people they can still connect with on an emotional level. In the tasks of daily life, our emotional needs often get pushed to the side and we stop seeing our spouse as an emotional being and more as a helper who helps us meet obligations and complete tasks. When this happens, it is very tempting to look for support elsewhere, and the marriage dies when you both stop trying to make it work.

Warning Signs You May Be Having An Emotional Affair

Perhaps you are not quite sure that you are having an emotional affair. If you are in a quandary, here are some signs that indicate you probably are:

You discuss very intimate topics, such as the troubles in your current relationship with this person, and you find yourself sharing almost all or at least most of your troubles and concerns with this person. As you do this, you also find yourself growing more discontent with your partner.

Frequent contact with the other person even when you are not together. You frequently in contact with this person even at questionable hours and spend a lot of time emailing, texting, or video calling this person.

This person consumes your thoughts and you think about him or her all the time. This other person is perhaps the first person you think about when you wake up in the morning, and he or she is on your mind when you go to sleep at night. You actually have this person in mind when you getting dressed, hoping they will notice your appearance.

You spend so much time together, and you find yourself creating reasons to spend time with them.

They the first person you want to call with any news, whether good or bad. You want them to rejoice with you when you have some exciting news to share or you want to lean on their shoulders for comfort when you have bad news. You may not even be sharing this news at all with your partner.

You believe that this person really gets you, feeling like he or she really understands you, and even does so better than your partner.

You start to keep secrets and to lie, which usually entails lying by omission. You intentionally do not tell your partner about your talks, lunches, meetings, phone calls and texts and are perhaps deleting messages from your phone that you do not want your partner to see. You may be denying the communication you had with him/her when asked, and may be hiding things or lying because you know deep down yourself that the behavior is not okay.

You often compare your partner to him or her, and may get angry with your partner for not doing things the way this other person does. Your partner starts to look bad in your eye and cannot quite measure up to this new friend of your's, and you may find yourself becoming more critical of your spouse.

Your partner gets less of you (in communication, affection, thoughts, time and focus) while this other special person gets more.

Signs Your Spouse Is Having An Emotional Affair

Here are some warning signs that your spouse is having an emotional affair:

- Your spouse starts withdrawing from you or criticizing you.

- Your spouse acts secretive or hides their phone, shuts down the computer screen suddenly when you are around.

- Your spouse seems interested in certain technology or hobbies seemingly out of the blue.

- Your spouse seems to always work extra hours on "project" with this friend.

- This friend of your spouse gets mentioned a lot. You seem to hear much about this person's opinions (and yours seems to count less and less)

- Your gut tells you something is going on. You are normally trusting and do not get jealous easily, but this definitely feels "off" to you.

- When you try to discuss any of these things with your partner, it is met with defensiveness or you are made to feel crazy.

DR. MYESHI WILLIAMS-BRILEY

NOTES

CHAPTER 2
THE IMPACT OF EMOTIONAL AFFAIRS: HOW DOES IT MAKE YOU FEEL?

As I briefly pointed out in the first chapter of this book, for most of us, the most hurtful and painful consequence of an emotional affair is the sense of being deceived, betrayed, and lied to.

Many social science researchers have studied the effects of affairs on those in relationships, and as can be expected, affairs can lead to rage and anger, depression, and loss of self-confidence or self-esteem. If you're the partner that is being cheated on in this way, whether it is a physical or emotional affair, it's very likely that you might experience extreme feelings of jealousy, anger, resentment and sadness. It's quite common for partners of cheaters to struggle with self-esteem issues. It is also natural to consider how you might not be living up to their expectations or hopes if you discover that your partner is emotionally involved with someone else.

Many partners that are dragged through infidelity often go through a time of shock or disbelief, and this is often followed by a lengthy grieving process, a grieving process that is not unlike what we feel when a loved one dies. You might go through denial, anger, sadness, and finally acceptance.

Husbands and wives need to understand what their partner considers cheating. Some might be okay with flirting with others while you are online gaming but others might consider this very disrespectful. This is why talking to each other and respecting each other's feelings is very important, in many different ways.

Here are some ways in which an emotional affair impacts the victim:

Rage and Anger

If there is a universal emotion that therapists see when infidelity has been discovered and exposed, it is anger. This might be anger at the spouse, at themselves, or at the whole world. Simply put, anger is a very common part of disclosure. This is because, if you didn't care, you would not be angry about it. We get angry because our heart has been broken.

Anger is basically a secondary emotion that is caused by other feelings. The roots of anger are resentment, soul wounds, inferiority complex, fear and righteous indignation.

First, an inability to eventually let go of resentment will frequently result in anger. If resentment is not properly released, it will lead to either anger or a perceived victim status. While it may be difficult to let go of resentments, doing so is a gift that you give yourself and this has very little to do with the other person. In the short term, it's a given that anger will be present and off the charts. However, as you journey towards finding help, and healing, and probably restoration, your anger must be diffused.

Personal soul wounds are also a significant source of anger. Each and every one of our past is littered with occurrences where the very core of our person was wounded and probably altered forever. This is also where we started to believe lies about our basic identity. The memories where these untruths are anchored can hold substantial amounts of pain and anger and when similar circumstances happen in the present, these old wounds come back to the surface and old emotions from the past echo, These have a great influence on how we feel in the present, and can be a great source of anger, causing our emotional responses to be larger-than-life.

When your hidden pain is triggered, you can have a thousand-dollar response to a one- dollar incident. If you discover that you tend to overreact to things, it might be worth your while to seek professional help to find out if there is a past wound inhibiting your ability to have peace in the present.

Inferiority complex is another root source of anger. This is because we have a very strange way of giving other people power over our personal lives. If we feel like we are being disrespected or when we feel inferior to another person, anger is often a common response. We do not like it when others fail to value us or affirm us, and when we feel undervalued, we tend to want to blame the other party. This response is even more exaggerated in the place of marriage. When you feel that your spouse treats you less than who you really are, your inferiority complex can become even worse when you find that they cheated.

Also, there are times when fear is at the root of anger. You are afraid of losing all that you have over the years built with your cheating spouse. Is he or she going to throw it all away for this new relationship in their lives? What would happen if they did?

Finally, most of the anger that emerges from a cheating incidence is rooted in righteous indignation. When a wrong has been committed and needs to be corrected, anger serves an intended purpose.

Lost Of Self Esteem Or Self Confidence

After the shock of learning that your partner had an affair has worn off, one of most painful after-effects is feeling as if you're not attractive, intelligent, or interesting. Your self-confidence that was in great shape just the day before the discovery is now shattered. You start to question your looks, wondering if they had been lying when they told you were beautiful or handsome. You doubt if you were a good sexual partner. You don't if you are as intelligent as you initially thought you were.

Jealousy

Jealousy is defined as an unpleasant emotion that arises when another person encroaches on something one feels is their own, and it can be particularly frustrating and difficult to talk about. It can happen in any kind of relationship but it is generally associated with romantically involved partnerships. Many cultures generally encourage monogamous relationships, and jealousy often stems from concerns or suspicions, (both legitimate and unfounded) that someone in the relationship is no longer faithful. If left unaddressed, jealousy can severely hinder a person's ability to communicate effectively.

Now imagine what this does to someone who finds out that their suspicions were actually true and that their partners cheated on them emotionally.

Research has now linked several traits to jealousy and these traits are low self-esteem, neuroticism (a general tendency to be moody, anxious, and emotionally unstable), feelings of insecurity and possessiveness and dependence on your partner. Jealousy is also linked with feelings of inadequacy in your relationship and an anxious attachment style which is a fear that your partner will leave you or won't love you enough.

Saddness

Sadness is emotional pain that is associated with, or that is characterized by, feelings of loss, disadvantage, despair, grief, disappointment, helplessness, and sorrow. It is that deep, dark feeling at the bottom of your belly that you cannot get rid of, especially when you think about the way your partner cheated on you.

Shame

Most of us expect ourselves to be angry if we ever discovered an affair, but why are you feeling shame? Shame is typically prompted by a sense of disgrace because a person believes that they made a mistake. So, it should be your partner feeling shame, right? Definitely not you. After all, they were the one that behaved badly.

But uncovering an affair makes you to evaluate yourself. We all have a tendency to wind and then rewind the movie reels of our lives, looking for blame; and we will often feel as if we had messed up somewhere. The thing is that you're not alone if you ever feel shame; most people who have been cheated on feel shame.

Emptiness

Feeling sad comes naturally after losing the affections of someone that you love, but emptiness is a different ballgame altogether because it is the absence of emotion. People are often petrified when they look inside themselves and realize there's nothing there, but you need to understand that a feeling of emptiness is really a psychological mechanism that kicks in when you are in shock. It actually protects the mind in some ways, and it usually dissipates given time and resolution of the trauma.

Possessiveness

You may have long told yourself that if your spouse ever cheated on you, you'd dump them in a heartbeat. This is a normal feeling that many people share. So why then, when you feel that your spouse has strayed, are you thinking about wanting him or her back more than ever? Separations between spouses can actually generate an increase in attraction, and your thoughts that your partner is in someone else's arms can birth a longing in you to pull you close together.

Annoyance

You will also, along with all the other very strong emotions that you as a betrayed partner might have to confront, feel a pervasive sense of irritation with what your spouse has done. As a partner, you will wonder how they could have been so stupid. You will be irritated that this stupid mistake of theirs now directly affects you. You had higher expectations for your spouse, and they didn't live up to expectation. Your spouse's behavior has now affected everything in your lives and this to you can be very irritating.

Relief

Many individuals who discover a spouse's affair had sensed that something was wrong, but had not been able to figure it out. Most of these people had been seeing signs of it for months and now that it's in the open, they can finally begin to work on it.

Rumination

Women in particular are likely to respond to their partners' cheating with a psychological practice termed "rumination" which is defined as the tendency to think repetitively about the causes, situational factors, as well as the consequences of a negative emotional experience. If you have ever been made to feel bad, rumination is that thing that makes you go over that feeling endlessly in your mind.

One of the reasons we tend to ruminate over a relationship gone awry is the addictive nature of love and the way we react to its betrayal or removal. Women are more likely to ruminate than men because, as one study found, women in general are likely to feel more responsibility for the "emotional tone" of relationships and for any negative events that occur in them than men. In other words, women are somewhat conditioned to believe it's at least partially their fault.

Paranoia

This one is not that unexpected, but it's certainly one of the most denied impact on those who have been cheated on. It is also of the most difficult impacts to get rid of. Without quite realizing it, being cheated on taints and stains your perceptions about relationships and keeps you in a perpetual mindset of mistrust and breach of trust. Cheating thus forces you to always have your guard up, and you may be unable to let down this guard even when things are going well. If care is not taken, it causes you to grow a hard exterior that is almost impossible to penetrate.

Behaviorial Changes

If you have been cheated on, the way you interact with your children or friends can change. Being cheated on will not just affect your self-worth and self-esteem; but it can also affect the manner in which you treat those around you. Pent up anger, hurt, or bitterness can show up in how you behave around the people you encounter. Trust is emotional and intimate and can be fully shattered by cheating. Your mental and physical body can take a huge hit from cheating and the feelings that come from this hit can inadvertently be transferred to all of your other relationships. It can unintentionally cloud every aspect of your life and this includes how you treat your kids, other family members, friends, and colleagues.

Guilt

This may initially sound backward. You have been cheated on and your trust has been violated by your partner, so why are you the one feeling guilty? But you feel guilty, nevertheless. You tell yourself you could have done more, been a better lover or caretaker or been more sensitive to his or her needs. You feel like this breakup is your fault.

Depression

In extreme cases, the partner of a cheating spouse may become depressed. Depression is actually a common medical illness that negatively impacts how you feel, the way you think and how you act. Depression causes feelings of sadness as well as a loss of interest in activities that you once enjoyed and can lead to a variety of emotional and physical problems than can limit a person's ability to function at home and at work.

Depression symptoms can range from very mild to severe and can include loss of interest or pleasure in activities once enjoyed, changes in appetite — weight loss or gain unrelated to dieting, trouble sleeping or sleeping too much, an increase in purposeless physical activity such as hand-wringing or pacing, slowed movements and speech, feeling guilty or worthless, difficulty in thinking, concentrating or making decisions. In extreme cases, depression can lead to thoughts of death or suicide.

It is important to note that depression is different from sadness or grief/bereavement. For example, the death of a beloved one, the loss of a job or the end of a relationship are traumatic experiences for an individual to endure. It is human for feelings of grief or sadness to develop in reaction to such situations. This grieving process is natural and exclusive to each individual and does share some of the same characteristics of depression, as both grief and depression involve sadness and withdrawal from usual day to day activities.

Depression however differs from sadness and grief in two major ways. First, in the case of grief, painful feelings come in waves, often intermixed with positive memories. In depression however, mood and/or interest (pleasure) are decreased for most of two weeks.

Also, in the case of grief, self-esteem is usually maintained. In depression, feelings of worthlessness and self-loathing are common.

DO YOU WANT CAKE OR CRUMBS IN YOUR MARRIAGE?

NOTES

CHAPTER 3
HOW STRONG IS AN EMOTIONAL AFFAIR?

An emotional affair is intensely strong even if it starts off as a platonic friendship. So, why is it many people rationalize that an 'emotional affair' is not truly a betrayal of their partner? Is it because this type of affair is often termed a 'non-physical' affair or an 'affair of the heart'?

But let's tell ourselves an unpleasant truth here; An affair is an affair, whether it is one of emotional infidelity or one of physical intimacy.

Check out these Bible verses: 1 Corinthians 13:13: "And now these three remain: faith, hope and love. But the greatest of these is love."

Song of Solomon 4:9: "You have captivated my heart, my sister, my bride; you have captivated my heart with one glance of your eyes, with one jewel of your necklace."

A non-physical affair makes up emotionally what it may lack sexually, and the entire relationship is constructed upon sharing sacred secrets with someone other than a partner. This itself is a clear warning sign when a married or committed person is seeking intimacy and looking to forge a connection to another person other than their significant other.

The cheating partner often justify their behavior, blaming it on feeling ignored or misunderstood or not in tune with their partner.

They manage to convince themselves that getting involved in an emotional affair is not as offensive as physical infidelity. On the contrary however, the betrayed partner often considers it more destructive to their person and to their marriage. They instinctively understand that there is a difference between physical and emotional intimacy and understand the true danger.

Dr. John Moore said it well. He says, "A tell-tale sign of an emotional affair is when a partner's emotional needs are met outside of the primary relationship." This is all encompassing. It goes right to the 'heart' of what an emotional affair truly is. If you are depending on another person to meet your emotional needs in any way, you have crossed that proverbial line and are no longer engaged in innocent banter and flirtation. You are not simply lending a sympathetic ear but are rather inviting a catastrophic domino effect on your relationship and your marriage.

We who live in the modern world have a harder battle to fight. We have the input of technology and social media to this type of infidelity. We send flirtatious texts and e-mails, and then we get together over a cup of coffee or lunch and get into the proper line of infidelity. The threat of this to a marriage or committed relationship is very much real.

These are the very real dangers of an emotional affair

The Increased Probability Of A Physical Affair

An emotional affair is often a foreplay for an actual physical affair. Statistically, these types of supposed 'friendships' more often than not leads to sexual affairs because the more secrets are shared, the more intimacy is developed. And the more intimacy develops, the more the bond is strengthened, and the more the bond is strengthened, the further the 'friendship' lines blur.

Moreover, these kinds of emotional affairs characteristically involve complaining about one's partner. This solidifies the cheating partner's need for empathy and this cements the affair even further. The cheating partner feels understood, and they soon begin to feel that these friendship of theirs is filling their emotional void. The cheating partner has found someone who understands him or her when they believe their partner no longer does.

The more this intimacy grows, the more likely a partner may feel connected and further daydream about this 'other' person.

The Further Deterioration Of Your Relationship

Whether an individual is dating or married, emotional infidelity will further endanger a relationship. This is because a healthy and happy couple is normally experiencing a sense of connectedness, and are in-tune and involved intimately with one another. However, it is an endangered relationship that is experiencing a time of detachment, disconnect and lack of emotional intimacy. It is this individual and/or couple that is at a higher risk for infidelity. This is why a person willing to connect with another person other than their partner is potentially endangering the entire future of a relationship that is already 'at risk'. This way, a compromised relationship becomes even more compromised, and the emotional intimacy in the relationship will decrease while the emotional distance increases.

This is a deadly manifestation in any relationship, as the most intimate connection an individual should experience is with their partner. The physical proximity of a relationship should match the emotional proximity, and an emotional affair just inserts another person between two spouses.

The Pollution Of Your Relationship

Both persons in a relationship need to protect that relationship by being very conscious of what they bring into their world. More often than not, unsatisfied and unhappy people believe that they deserve to have comfort outside of their marriage, forgetting the fact they made a commitment to become one in their relationship and not two.

Protecting a relationship means that you need to protect your partner and not just yourself. Simply put, deception, dishonesty, betrayal, and secrets are relationship pollutants. So why on earth would anyone want to gamble with toxic ingredients that will destroy their relationship? A non-physical affair has too much toxic relationship pollutants and it is often difficult to clean up.

DR. MYESHI WILLIAMS-BRILEY

The Six Stages of Emotional Affairs

Stage 1: You feel inadequate and unappreciated

At this point, you feel inadequate and experience fear that leads to resentment toward your wife or husband. You are drawn to the person who validates you because he or she reassures you that you are good and adequate. At this point, the other person understands your frustrations with your spouse and comforts you by listening and complimenting you. At this point, he or she may provide suggestions on how to help your marriage, and may give you ideas such as buying flowers and gifts. He or she may guide you on what to say or not say to help make things better.

As a result, you feel understood and calmer and you associate these good feelings with the other person. What you fail to realize is that the other person has effectively (whether knowingly or unknowingly) set the stage for emotional intimacy that you lack with your spouse.

Meanwhile, what is missing from your relationship is the ability to validate and attentively listen to your spouse and the importance of identifying and verbalizing positive aspects in the relationship.

Stage 2: You want more sex and feel sexually deprived

At this point, you feel rejected by your wife/ husband and do not feel desired by them anymore. On the other hand, this other person makes you feel alive by flirting, alluding to your sexuality and engaging your senses. For example, he or she touches your arm and tells you your spouse is lucky to have you. As a result of this, you want more attention from the other person in order to feel sexually attractive and this leads you to focus more on your appearance. When you are with your wife or husband, you are confused because you are feeling sexual tension towards your emotional affair partner, and you begin to create reasons to have more contact with other person by texting and calling him or her, looking at his/her social media photos, creating fake profiles and friending them.

Meanwhile, this person knows that you are susceptible and enjoys the attention and desire that you are demonstrating toward him/her, and continues to encourage you by flirting more. She or he might either coyly or brazenly touch your arm, wear a fragrance he or she knows that you like, bring you coffee or food and many more little treats. This person at this point enjoys the feeling of being in control of your desire for him or her.

Stage 3: Feeling bored with your spouse

Many men who cheated on their wives admitted to being bored within the relationship. When love is not actively cultivated, it is easy to begin to view your spouse as nothing more than a roommate. Meanwhile, this other person is creating stories that enhance your visual experience of fantasy, fun, and play. You are preoccupied with this other person and even when your spouse notices and points out this preoccupation, you respond defensively by saying "we are just friends." But deep in your heart, you are beginning to feel that you would have more fun in your life if this other person could just replace your spouse. They are more fun, they get you, and they make you laugh like your spouse has not made you do in a long time.

At this point, this couple is no longer working to share pleasant activities and have fun together on a regular basis. While this may sound like a cliché, consistently setting time aside for "date night" is a much-needed nurturing tool for the health of a relationship.

Stage 4: You want to talk but you feel that your spouse is unavailable

Relationships are tough and require work. For example, when a man calls his wife, she might be busy with the children, commitments, work, and can't talk; or the wife is resentful for doing the major portion of child-rearing and housekeeping and has no time to talk to him. On the other hand, she might call him and find that he is too busy with important work and urgent meetings to take the time to talk to her. Meanwhile, there is this other person that is becoming more available and who provides you with the company and friendship you are seeking. Because of this, this other person becomes your companion on the phone, in chat rooms, or face to face. This person doesn't even have to make any demands on you because they are already controlling you and your actions.

This is why it is important to be mindful of when you are both drifting apart and disconnecting in your marriage. It takes active participation in a relationship to notice and to listen to your instincts when you feel this and to understand that there is a difference between healthy autonomy and emotional distancing. Healthy autonomy is having a sense of self-identity that strengthens your relationship; while emotional distancing is more or less living separate lives and being emotionally disconnected from your spouse.

Stage 5: You feel like your spouse is making too many demands on you

At this stage of your emotional affair, you feel controlled and not trusted due to your spouse's questioning and checking on you, by looking at your phone or other devices. And then you choose to avoid your spouse's suspicions and regain control by using "burner numbers" or other methods of communication to maintain contact with the other person. You start to lie more frequently and make excuses to be further apart from your spouse in order to be closer to the other person. You now feel alive with adrenaline, and the rush of secrecy combined with fear excites you and you become increasingly addicted to the emotional affair because you no longer feel bored, undesired, or inadequate. You now want to have sex with this other person. He or she might oblige you or not.

Stage 6: You feel guilty and do not want to hurt your spouse

At this point, you now feel conflicted about having the emotional affair and you realise that it has never been your intention to hurt your spouse. You may share your guilt with this other person by saying things like, "I don't want to hurt her, I should not be doing this." Most of the time, this other person will tell you that you need to stop seeing each other because they also feel guilty and you immediately agree to this suggestion to relieve your guilt. You direct your energy toward your marriage; but this other person more often than not regenerates contact with you after some time spent apart. He or she might send random messages or make an unnecessary excuse to see you and the relationship hits off again.

In most cases of emotional affair which eventually led to divorce, this other person will at this time become more strategic with their connection, knowing that you are susceptible to break it off with them. They may resort to more aggressive means by having sex with you or enticing you with sexting, contacting your spouse and becoming friends with them, or expressing their love for you.

At this point, your guilty feelings increase and your obsessive yearning for the emotional affair generates the adrenaline rush of addictive behaviors to relieve your anxiety.

NOTES

DR. MYESHI WILLIAMS-BRILEY

CHAPTER 4
IS MY MARRIAGE REPAIRABLE AND DO I EVEN WANT TO REPAIR IT?

Is it possible for a relationship whose trust has been violated through cheating to survive and move past the cheating? The answer is yes. Your marriage is repairable, as long as both you and your spouse are ready to work on the relationship and move forward from the affair.

I have long said that if you or your partner has cheated through an emotional affair, it does not have to mean the end of your relationship. In fact, a breach of trust like this can provide you the opportunity to evaluate how you feel about your partnership, and it can be an opportunity to recognize an unhealthy pattern and decide to walk away. But if you want to work it out and use it to improve your relationship, there are steps that the person who emotionally cheated can take.

Steps To Be Taken By The Cheater To Repair A Marriage

Recognize the fantasy
Affairs exist in the infatuation phase, where brain chemistry goes crazy and makes you believe you've found your soul mate. This type of feeling is intoxicating, and it's important for the cheating partner to realize that they've been making decisions based on the drug of that neurological reaction. Emotional affair partners aren't real in the sense that you are not dealing with real life, with the stresses and

negative attributes that would show up later. You've been indulging in a dream. As appealing as it may have been, you can let it go more easily if you accept that it's been a mirage.

Distinguish romance from love

You need to understand that the romance you feel in your emotional affair is very different from real love. The truth is that, in when we yearn for a forbidden, passionate romance, we are often blinded to the beautiful, committed love that is with us in everyday life. While your every day love may not be exactly exciting or thrilling, you must understand that it and represents a willingness to share ordinary things in an extraordinary way, to find meaning in the simple, unromantic tasks. These are the things that build a life and a marriage.

Learn self-validation

Many people get involved with someone new because they are looking for positive reflection and attention. When you are missing that in your primary relationship and don't know how to validate yourself, it can be especially easy to find it somewhere else. It's important to develop the ability to feel good about yourself without needing external validation.

It probably goes without saying, but it's also important to improve your relationship with your partner so it's infused with positive attention and interaction. Consider where, how, or why you feel this lack, be open with your partner about how you feel, and try to work toward a solution together that helps you feel secure and loved—without placing the full burden on your partner to change.

Cut off ties with the other person

This is the time to focus on your relationship and not risk the slippery slope anymore. In order to earn trust with your partner, there should be no contact with the third person that isn't required (for work and such). Splitting your attention and continuing to siphon some of your energy to the other person just keeps the dynamic going. Be clear that you are ending it (both with the third person and with your partner), and be willing to demonstrate that by being transparent with your communication mechanisms (social media, email, etc.).

Confront the deceit

The worst part about affairs is the breach of trust, the willingness one partner shows to disregard the feelings and experience of the other. The person who had the emotional affair needs to wrestle with the fact that they were willing to lie to their partner and hide what was happening. Share exactly what happened and when, to the degree that the resolute partner wants to know. Examine the extent of the dishonesty and the prevalence of lying in your life in general. Commit to speaking the truth and being transparent from now on.

Outsmart the body

Let's take a little biology lesson. When you are besotted with someone, your brain chemistry tells you some lies that can have you doing really stupid stuff that you would not normally do. You will experience a rise in dopamine and norepinephrine and these will lead to heightened sexual tension. You start to feel that all your troubles would go away if you only kissed that beautiful babe you just met through Facebook, or if you sat across the table and gazed into the eyes of that new secretary of yours.

A simple truth here: Love is a drug and the region in your brain that it stimulates is the same region affected when you snort cocaine. You therefore need to identify the physiological components of infatuation in order to fight and win the war against infidelity.

Treat the addiction

Putting an emotional affair in the same category as an addiction is helpful in two ways: First, it strips your person from the experience, making it easier to let go of, and it also provides you with some tangible steps that you can take to kick the habit. Addictions induce in humans a trance-like state that allows you to detach from the guilt, pain, and shame that you feel and you buy into false and empty promises until reality hits.

Give yourself the permission to grieve

A relationship without sex can just be as intense as one involving sex, and you might need to grieve the special connection that you had or felt you had with this other person in order to move forward.

In the case of emotional affairs, guilt can hinder the grieving process because you feel as though you were wrong to have had these feelings to begin with and you don't often won't allow the time of tears and grief that are necessary for healing.

That the relationship happened outside of your committed relationship does not mean that your heart isn't broken and doesn't need to heal. So be gentle with yourself.

DR. MYESHI WILLIAMS-BRILEY

Surround yourself with friends

Friends aren't optional for a person who has just gotten out of an emotional affair. You need to recognize that they are a life-support system, especially important if your emotional relationship happened at work among mutual friends. You will need to befriend friends who are not connected to the other person in any way, or you might have to hang out with your non-work friend until you feel emotionally strong enough to socialize with mutual friends who might talk about or involve this other person.

Be accountable

Accountability works for someone who has cheated on their partner when he or she has a few people in their lives who can question them if they are still on the straight and narrow path. Your accountability partner can be your therapist, my doctor, your mentor, your parent, your sibling or your best friend. By giving them the lowdown on what's really going on in your head decreases your margin for error.

Recommit to making your relationship work

Emotional affairs often sprout from the fertile ground of relationship dissatisfaction. Now is the time to figure out where the two of you have been struggling and how to recreate your relationship now so that both of you can get your needs met. Consider seeing a couple's therapist or taking a workshop together. Work through relationship self-help books to strengthen your foundation. Talk honestly about your wants, needs, and complaints. An affair can put your relationship on the brink; this is the time to lay it all out there and address all the problems.

Invest heavily in your marriage

The best way to stop an affair from happening is to invest in your marriage. Also, the best way to recover from an affair is to invest heavily in your marriage. This is a simple physics equation: the time and energy you give to one relationship must come from another one. You cannot build and nurture a true relationship if you are spreading intimacy in too many places.

After a violation of trust, the best reconciler in a relationship are often the small acts of kindness. For most partners, "I'm sorry" doesn't do a thing, and your regret needs to be supported with evidence such as special dinners, cleaning toilets, backrubs, and a listening ear.

Know that trust will take time

You don't heal from an affair just because it ends and the offending partner apologizes. The person who had the affair has shown an ability to lie and hide things. It's normal to struggle with trust, and there may be strong emotions (including both sadness and anger) for quite a while. What will move you through this is a combination of time and demonstrated change. The cheating partner needs to be trustworthy if they are going to earn trust. You both need to see that there is a new level of honesty, an ability to bring up and address unmet needs, and a recommitment to the partnership. Whatever laid the groundwork for the affair has to change, and that means both people have work to do to make sure the relationship is fulfilling to the other.

Affairs, both of the emotional and sexual varieties, are painful. But they can also be the impetus to tackle long-standing problems and transform your relationship for the better. If what you see is a fatal flaw of dishonesty or lack of commitment, use the affair as a chance to find a better relationship. But if you believe that yours is worth saving, take this as an opportunity to make important growth as a person and as a partner.

DO YOU WANT CAKE OR CRUMBS IN YOUR MARRIAGE?

NOTES

CHAPTER 5
CAN A MARRIAGE SURVIVE AN EMOTIONAL AFFAIR?

In the previous chapter, we examined what it would take on the cheater's part if a marriage is to survive an emotional affair. But it is important to understand that the bulk doesn't stop there. The one who has been cheated on also has his or her part to play in order for the marriage to survive.

Key Actions You Can Take To Help Repair Your Relationship

There must be genuine repentance and remorse

There needs to be genuine repentance. Your partner has to feel deeply sorry and this can't be something that should come off casual. You have to make sure that there is a deep sense of regret and remorse for what happened. This may require your partner to open up and be honest about why the emotional affair happened. Infidelity is very complex, and there's much depth and intricacy as to why people cheat and there is no hard and fast rule as to how you can find your way back to each other. This is why it is important to find out what was it in your relationship that ultimately caused you to open the door for a third party to walk into it. Gaining this insight into your relationship is incredibly important.

If cheating partner is not willing to be upfront about the reason it happened or if he or she starts pointing blame, patching things might be impossible. He or she cannot give an oversimplified reason such as 'I'm a man' or 'it wasn't planned. It just happened", as the only way to rebuild trust is to be completely clear why it happened so when faced with a similar situation in the future, a different choice will be made.

Don't take it personally

Since you've discovered your partner's emotional infidelity and his or her reason for it, odds are that you have spent a whole lot of time thinking about what you could've done differently. Perhaps if you had had more sex, if you had watched all his games, or listened to her complaints about work and done something about it, then maybe your wife or husband wouldn't have gone out to find someone else. Yes, emotional affairs don't happen in a void and there is often some level of distancing between spouses that opens up gives a third party a chance to come in. Despite this, you need to understand that your partner's affair is not your fault. It would have happened anyway, as long as your partner was willing to allow it. So, don't take it personally.

Get some help processing it

There is one other thing that you must do after learning about an emotional affair, and this is to get help processing it. Friends are a great source of support, as they are definitively on your side but they might not give you the best advice that you need to move forward.

It is imperative that you seek out the help of a therapist or a life coach to help you through the difficult times as you wrestle with guilt, sadness, shame, anger, fear, and many other unexpected emotions.

This is because these emotions can fester for a long time if you don't deal with them, and getting past it will be more difficult for you.

After an affair, it is often hard to know what to do and where to start. It is possible that the conversations you are having with your spouse feel like they are not getting anywhere; this is where a licensed therapist can help guide the process. The therapist's is a neutral party to the conversation and this neutrality helps identify what underlying needs are unmet and how these needs can be processed within the couple's relationship. This is an investigative stage of therapy, and it offers couples the opportunity to seek understanding, discover compassion, have a better ability to problem-solve and to move forward.So, reach out and get some professional help right now.

Remember to take care of yourself

When we go through emotionally tough times, we are inclined to take one of two directions: We either feel drained of all energy and want to do nothing more than sit with the remote and binge watch while eating junk food. Or we might push ourselves really hard to be more productive and get things done. Both of these reactions are meant to numb the pain that we feel, and they are both extreme reactions. It is best to consciously settle somewhere in the middle and never forget to take care of yourself.

Here is how to take care of yourself.

Make sure you get quality sleep every night. If you are finding it hard to sleep, find something that will help you do. This is because it will be harder to deal with your difficulties if you are also running low on sleep.

Try to eat more of balanced meals instead of indulging in junk food.

Make sure to get your heart rate up every day by exercising, or taking a walk or dancing around your home. Getting your heart rate up is a great way to deal with the stress you are under, as the dopamine your body generates from the exercise helps to smooth out your emotions.

Be choosy about who you tell

Your instantaneous reaction might be to tell the whole world about your partner's indiscretions and paste it across social media for all to see, and this is a common coping mechanism. Many people go to extreme lengths to hurt their spouse in a very public manner and this is often done out of anger and with lack of lucidity that usually makes the spouse who was actually cheated on look bad or crazy because of their extreme reaction. It's required that you talk to someone about what is going on in your life, but telling every single person in your inner circle can come back to bite you.

The more people you tell, the more people will have their opinions based off of simply trying to protect you from getting further hurt. These kinds of coalitions and loyalties amongst friends and family members may make moving forward problematic, especially if you and your spouse decide to work on your relationship. You may be able to forgive and move on, but your friends and family will keep on holding on to an intense grudge that will put more pressure on an already susceptible relationship that is trying its best to rebuild and move on.

DR. MYESHI WILLIAMS-BRILEY

Things To Avoid As You And Your Partner Rebuild Your Relationship

Following a major breach of trust in your relationship, it might feel like an uphill battle to move on as a couple. And the truth is that it is. But if you and your spouse decide to stay together after emotional cheating, and work on things, rebuild your trust, and walk through this rough patch together, you certainly can. What it takes is effort, time, and a knowledge of the most common mistakes that couples make after a breach of trust.

As someone who has been cheated on, here are the things you must avoid if you want to rebuild your relationship:

Keeping your feelings all to yourself

Although you might not want to tell every single person in your life that you're having relationship problems, it's still not a great idea to keep these relationship issues a full secret, either. This is extremely harmful because it puts pressure on your relationship and forces both you and your partner to present to others as though nothing is wrong. You need to discuss your feelings with a loved one or a licensed therapist to start the healing process.

Asking your partner for all the small details

Even if you are dying to know exactly how the betrayal happened, where it happened, what went down, etc., asking your partner for all the little details is never a good idea. Rather than make you feel better, you will probably feel worse because you now have very vivid images of your spouse having an emotional connection and possibly sleeping in the same bed with this other person, and that is an image that's difficult to shake. Make sure ask questions and get the details that you need to know. But you must resist the urge to learn every single thing because having too many details can make moving on difficult and very painful

Not talking about the problems at all

All of that said, you cannot simply go on with your lives and act like the cheating incident didn't happen. This does nothing but slow down the recovery process, so it is important that you and your partner are open in talking about your different experiences and the emotions you felt about the betrayal in trust. This provides a means to process your emotions and continue moving forward. If you don't talk about it, you most likely will get stuck in resentments, anger, sadness, and unvoiced feelings

Minimizing the impact it had

When you talk about it, be honest about the impact this infidelity has had on you. Cheating in any form can make the spouse who was cheated on feel totally insecure and you have to tell your partner when you are feeling insecure this way and what they can do in order to make you feel better.

Getting even

One of the hugest mistakes you can make is trying to get even with your spouse, by going out and paying them in their own coin by also cheating or breaching trust. Try to resist this urge if you have it, because getting even leaves no room for regret, reconnection, and repair.

Holding a grudge

Anytime your trust is brutally betrayed, you may find it hard to ever truly forget, and I am not asking you to try to force your brain to delete what happened. I am however asking you to try your best not to hold a grudge. Holding a grudge means that you may continually take it out on your partner, treating them unfairly and making it difficult to reestablish your relationship on solid ground.

Being suspicious and paranoid

If your partner breached your trust, it makes all the sense in the world that you'd feel paranoid or suspicious, and be tempted to take a closer look at what they do or say to make sure it doesn't happen again.

But doing this excessively will only further harm the trust in this relationship. This is because true trust demands that couples tolerate what they don't know about their partners. Also, intimacy can easily be killed by these attempts at control.

Trying to reestablish trust in one fell swoop

Don't make the mistake of expecting trust to be regained immediately, as this will take time. You might, for example, be okay with your spouse going out with friends at night after an affair has been exposed, but maybe not him or her going away for an entire weekend.

It is important that you both understand the difference, and to understand that trust is incremental and takes time to grow.

Trying to heal yourself all by yourself

If you plan to work things out and remain a couple, you will have to learn to lean on each other during this difficult time, same way you would during any other tough times. It is not uncommon for people to try to go it alone, but it is wrong

It is often unnoticed that the offending partner is hurting, too. For example, they may have very sensible grievances that, although not justifying the emotional affair, need to be addressed. You need to be there for each other as much as is possible, as this will make it easier to move on.

Making your whole relationship about the affair

Some couples, after the discovery of an affair, build their entire relationship around that affair. This affair becomes the sun that their world together revolves around, and they fail to incorporate the affair into their total narrative. This is a terrible thing to do to a struggling relationship. It is important to know that it will be difficult to move on if the infidelity becomes the only conversation in your relationship.

Becoming obsessive about what went wrong

You will be tempted to figure out and fix what went wrong, and to discover which mistakes led up to the affair. But that, if done obsessively, can be a mistake. Infidelity doesn't mean the relationship was bad. There is this societal theory that partner cheats only if they are unhappy in their relationship or their spouse is not fulfilling them in some way. The truth though is that many people cheat even when they are in very happy and satisfying relationships. This said, you need to give yourself a break, and be okay with not getting to the very bottom of things.

Expecting things to return to normal right away

The process of recovery from an affair is likely to be a lengthy one, and you need to be okay with that. Far too often, people put a limit on their healing and will say stuff like 'it's been four months already, I should be over it'. The truth is that there is no timeframe for healing from an infidelity, and placing a time frame on healing actually hinders going through the whole process of healing and recovery. You also need to recognize that you and your spouse might have different trajectories in healing.

Failing to design a plan

One of the biggest mistake couples make after infidelity is to reconcile without a solid accountability plan. You need to address issues such as what you need your partner to do in order to feel secure and how you plan to support each other for this not to happen again

Playing the victim card

Yes, you didn't deserve to have your partner cheat on you, but this doesn't mean you should just sit there and wallow in self-pity. This is because playing the victim will keep you feeling damaged and helpless, and will continue to keep you feeling terrible about yourself. This will make your self-esteem drop further, and you'll find it hard to get on with your life in a fulfilling way.

Getting the children involved

If you have kids, do your best to keep these precious ones out of it until absolutely necessary. The cheating situation should stay between you and spouse. Otherwise, it puts children in a situation where they may feel they have to make a choice between the two of you. And only give children information on a need-to-know basis only, and make sure you keep assuring them that you all will survive this situation.

Letting someone else decide if you will leave or not

Every single person you tell about the affair will have their own opinion as to what you should do. Some will tell you to give your spouse another chance and some will ask you to leave him or her immediately. But it's your choice and your choice alone whether the relationship is worth repairing or not. You alone know what's best for yourself.

Trying to get things back to how they were before the affair

Your marriage is already changed, and the way that things were is what led you two to the situation at hand. Something needs to transform going forward if you are to keep your relationship strong and healthy. This is why you should focus on building a more fulfilling relationship by incorporating the lessons you've learned. Instead of looking backward, create a new chapter, repair the dysfunctional undercurrents, and come out of it as a stronger, more connected couple.

Forgetting to take care of yourself

This distressing experience can impact your mind and body negatively. To bounce back from this, you must understand that self-care is vital. You can't make cogent decisions, such as whether you stay or leave, when you are not taking care of your basic needs. So, make sure that you sleep, eat, exercise, and have fun. As much as you can, laugh and live a happy life in spite of what's going on. Go for coping techniques such as therapy, writing in a journal, meditation, hanging with supportive friends, or reading self-help books.

NOTES

CHAPTER 6
WHAT CAN I DO TO HEAL MYSELF FOR THE FUTURE?

There is nothing in this world that can prepare you for the emotional destruction that falls on you when you discover that the one you love, the one who was supposed to love you right back, and the one you built your whole life with, has betrayed you.

After discovering that your partner has been cheating on you, you will be shaken to the very core by a storm of emotions. You will be grieving, angry, broken-hearted, confused, and most of all, deeply hurt. And if you have friends and close family members who want you to move past the hurt, you'll probably hear sayings of comfort such as, "Time heals all wounds." This saying is not helpful, and it certainly is also not true.

Time all on its own, will not teach you how to heal your broken heart and get your life back on track after you catch your partner cheating. It's what you personally do with the time that you have that will determine whether you will find healing after the heartbreak of infidelity, or whether you carry your wounds into your future relationships and life.

It doesn't really matter what your particular circumstances are or what you're feeling in your heart, if you are suffering from the aftermath of your cheating partner's affair and want to take charge of mending your broken heart, there is hope for you.

It is not exactly easy to heal from the trauma of betrayal and learn to feel genuinely happy and peaceful again, but it is doable.

Tips On How To Heal Your Broken Heart After Catching Your Spouse Cheating

See from a higher and different perspective

I am inviting you to look at what has happened in a way that will bring you peace of mind and release you from unnecessary suffering. I am inviting you to look at your situation using the "eyes" of the soul, as this will allow you start to comprehend why this betrayal took place on a deeper level.

I am inviting you to understand that nothing in this life is random, and that everything that happens in your life, even this heartache, is specifically designed for your learning and growth. I am inviting you to see this challenging and painful event as a learning opportunity. Perhaps it is an opportunity to heal your deepest emotional wounds, those thoughts, judgments and beliefs that have held you back since you were a child.

I am inviting you to accept that there is a spiritual reason for the betrayal, and that the creator is neither unkind nor random, but has your back at all times. Trust that He is looking out for you.

Feel and move through your feelings

When a partner cheats, many couples begin to work with therapists to get the healing process started. Talking about how you feel is necessary to process them but when you add the power of your body to literally move through the overwhelming feelings, you can really ramp up your healing.

For example, conscious breathing instantly lowers your heart rate and respiration and diffuses your fight or flight response. When you add body-centered processes like breathing and dance (among others), your healing comes much more easily.

Think better thoughts

Your thoughts are the things that fuel almost all your pain, and you will start feeling better when you discover the negative, inner dialogue that energizes your upset. You will feel better when you re-write the false stories you have made up about yourself as a fallout of being betrayed. To uncover and then update certain beliefs about yourself is one of the most personally transformative work you can do.

When you focus on your thoughts and acknowledge which ones are causing you pain, it is certain that peace will soon follow.

Heal your relationship with your partner and with yourself

You need to heal your relationship with your partner, whether you decide to stay or go. This is because even if the physical relationship with your partner ends, you will still have a relationship with your partner in your mind forever.

The collective feelings and thoughts you have about a being create your inner experience of that individual, irrespective of whether they are in your life every day, or if you have not seen them in ten years. You hold a space for everyone you have ever encountered in your thoughts, and it is these thoughts that create your feelings.

While it is challenging, you surely have the power to change your thoughts, and it is your choice what you will experience every time that you think about a particular person, your partner included.

Reclaim your power

No matter what you are feeling about yourself was before the emotional affair, when your spouse betrays you, it will feel like your world has been unhinged. You will feel like you've been chopped to your knees and stripped of your power. In order to recover fully, you first need to understand just how you gave your power away before the affair and after it, and how to get that power back. You might have given your power away by investing too much of your time and energy in the relationship and neglecting yourself, (codependency), when you didn't speak your truth, when you didn't set boundaries and when you projected your own issues onto your partner.

Reclaim your power, and your healing will begin.

Let it go when forgiving seems impossible

The best way to start to find peace and healing is to learn that it is your judgments that is driving your un-forgiveness. When you release these judgments. whether they are of yourself or others, you get to truly move beyond the pain of betrayal. This is not the same thing as traditional forgiveness, because I am asking you to begin with self- forgiveness before you consider forgiving another.

DR. MYESHI WILLIAMS-BRILEY

Uncomfortable Things To Come To Terms With So You Must Heal

You couldn't have stopped it

You will write and rewrite your past. You will begin with certain days, certain afternoons, certain trips, trying to identify the points where you could have changed the timeline, could have prevented a meeting, swayed his or her gaze. You will want to find the gaps where you could have stopped it. You will want, absurdly, to take responsibility, to square off the pain a bit, make yourself feel complicit.

The sad truth is that we give too much, even when we're grieving. The reality you need to know now is that you couldn't have stopped it. You couldn't have worn a sexier bra, gave more of yourself, been more aware of his (or her) texting habits. You couldn't have worked harder to retract their decision. You need to understand and accept that the decision to cheat was your partner's; it wasn't yours.

You will not trust your partner for a while

Some people move on from cheating and infidelity rather quickly. Some of us, however, cannot so easily let a cheater go. We are the people who love deeply and fully, who honor our partners, who see love (and sex) as sacred, lasting things, infinite, terrifying, primal.

Infidelity is the seven-layer wound that will eradicate your trust and for a time, love will disgust you. Your trust will run away from you, even when you want so badly to trust them with the whole of your heart. Understand that this is normal, and that it is fundamental to your healing.

You can't stop it from happening again. In fact, your partner may do it again

You may encounter infidelity again, even when you regift your trust and are ready to love and be loved honestly and fully. If you do stay with the partner who cheated on you, you need to understand that he or she may not remain faithful. Infidelity is not something that you can cut up yourself on. There is no checklist that you can follow to prevent it. All you can do is love.

It is not always the other person's fault

It is natural to want to villainize the other person involved with your partner and this is very easy to do. Often, we turn that complicit lover into a demon, imagining the person to be a dark, seductive, tempting, smarter, sexier, richer, more successful lover, one who is better than you in all ways.

However, you need to realize that you may be wrong. There are still people out there who will refuse to engage in an affair with your partner if they know that he or she is already in a relationship. Of course, there are also those who will not refuse.

You also need to realize that there are those who are hurting and those who are deceived, unhappy, and looking for validation just as we all are. As much as you want to blame the other person, I encourage you not to. Most of the time, there is simply not enough information to correctly assign blame.

It is not you that needs to change

In the wake of infidelity, you may stop eating then eat a lot. You may find yourself obsessing over new clothing lines, changing the way you speak and what you speak about. Part of this will be fueled by the desire to fumble your way closer to a true and authentic, unfazed you. Part of it will be egged on by a profound, dynamic kind of anger.

But a huge part of it would be your belief that you could change yourself to prevent this from happening again. This is because we humans are very good at thinking that we are solely responsible for our wounds.

Get this right; You are not the person who needs to change. Your cheating partner always is. You also need to realise that he or she may not ever change because changing is a personal choice.

Make the changes that you need to heal, but please do not only make them for the sake of infidelity. Make them to become a better person.

You may never know why

That you may never know why your partner cheated is perhaps the hardest truth you will have to face.

If you are like any of us, you probably want to know why he or she had an emotional affair. You may have already asked why and received an answer or not. Some cheaters are sex addicts; some are abusers; some are misogynists; and some are narcissists. Others are confused and lonely, looking for something even they can't even identify.

The truth is that you may never know why he or he cheated. But you must move on, nonetheless.

DR. MYESHI WILLIAMS-BRILEY

NOTES

CHAPTER 7
HEALING YOUR MARRIAGE

There is work to be done if you are to heal your marriage. Most relationships (marriages) start off with great communication and great sex, and once one of these components begin to slack in the relationship, both partners are opening the door for possible cheating.

I am therefore dedicating this last chapter to these two important components of marriage and I want to encourage anyone reading this book who has not yet experienced the heartache of their partner cheating on them (whether physically or emotionally) to work on these aspects of their marriage as a security deposit on never having cheating happen.

And if cheating has already happened in your relationship and both you and your partner are working things out, here are two components you must work on.

As we go through this last chapter together, I want you to bear these in mind;

Ephesians 4:2: "Be completely humble and gentle; be patient, bearing with one another in love."

1 Peter 4:8: "Above all, love each other deeply, because love covers over a multitude of sins."

DR. MYESHI WILLIAMS-BRILEY

John 15:12: "My command is this: Love each other as I have loved you."

Communication

There is hardly any married couple that does not want to live happily ever after, but about half of all legal marriages in the United States end in divorce, simply because couples do not know how to communicate. And because of this, small disagreements build up over time and splinter the relationship.

There is more to having a happy relationship than talking about what's bothering us; it matters more to do the talking thoughtfully.

But we don't have these thoughtful conversations. We're afraid to talk about how we're going to have deep conversations in our relationships, and very often, this results in individuals not knowing what's a big thing and what's a little issue that should be ignored. We don't know the best way to bring up the big things, and the best way to tackle the little issues.

Marriages don't end overnight and when people end up in divorce attorneys' offices, it's usually because of problems like infidelity or financial impropriety. These big problems however are often the consequence of small misunderstandings that were not resolved and that have snowballed over time.

For example, a marriage might begin to fall apart after the kids come and the husband starts making small jokes about her weight. He might think that he is being playful but, in reality, these are really cutting to her. When someone hurts us, the go-to-reaction and inclination is to hurt them back. Failing this, we start to lose affection for them. Both of these scenarios create distance.

As the couple feels less and less affectionate towards one another, there is ultimately a gradual breakdown in communication over time until it is no longer existent.

These are little things that are not intended to be hurtful. They're not intended to destroy a marriage, but it is important to note that no single rain drop is responsible for a flood. When communication lags and then stops, little things add up to the opposite of love, until partners feel disconnected from each other and unsupported.

How To Have More Thoughtful Dialogue With Your Partner

Use positive reinforcement

Our instinct is to criticize the person we love when we are upset with them. And while our purpose is to improve them in some way and make them better versions of themselves, our criticism often results in them feeling ashamed or slighted. It doesn't matter if it is called constructive criticism; it is still criticism, and no one likes to be criticized. This is especially true when it comes to marriage. Criticism in marriage is like being told, 'You're not doing this marriage thing right,' or 'You suck at being my spouse.'"

Resist the urge to criticize your partner if you want to change their behavior, and focus instead on praising those things that they do that make you happy. For example, watch your partner's behavior for acts of selflessness and praise them for this if you want your spouse to be more selfless. Let them know how much you like it.

When you praise like this, it will inspire your partner in a positive way as opposed to having him or her feel attacked.

DR. MYESHI WILLIAMS-BRILEY

Focus on principles when arguing

When couples are in a verbal disagreement, they usually try to reach a common ground but more often than not, neither of them gets what they want at the end of the day. They go back and forth until maybe they get to some middle ground between their respected positions, and this middle position almost rewards each of them taking an unreasonable starting position.

Let's take example, if your spouse says something underhanded about your brother that you don't like, you might respond instinctively by criticizing one of his siblings too. You're not actually upset at your spouse for saying something about your brother in an offhanded comment. Rather, you are mad because you feel he or she is being disrespectful to your brother and worry he or she doesn't like your brother, so you reach out and disrespect his sibling to even the score.

You shouldn't do this. Instead, get to the very core of the matter. Instead of attacking your spouse for what he or she said, talk to him or her about why his/her sentence bothered you in the first place.

Write an email or a text

Our culture puts great importance on conducting difficult conversations on a face-to-face sit across the table from each other basis, but confronting your partner about something they did in person has a greater chance of putting them in a defensive position, and you are unable to resolve the matter.

What more, your spouse may not be in a position where he or she really wants to talk about that issue right at the moment that you are.

If your partner has offended you in some way, try to express how you feel in a carefully worded email or text. This is great because it gives them the opportunity to reflect on the matter and think about how to respond in a non-confrontational way.

Good Sex

Can you remember those hungry, lusty days when your relationship was new? The sex was better than good; it was delicious, and you almost always wanted and had a second (and perhaps third and fourth) helping. If you are in a long-term relationship. you will notice the difference between your sex life then and now, and if you are not very careful, you might think that the huge difference spells nothing but doom for your relationship.

Don't be dismayed, and please know that you are not alone. It has been proven that decreasing sexual intimacy is the reality for many long-term relationships.

You will come to a point in your relationship when you get past the infatuation and discovery phase. At this point, you are secure with each other and you find that life's stresses and your everyday obligations start to become more of a priority. Many external stressors and factors like work, commutes, parenting or chores will threaten being in 'the mood' for sex even though you are still in love with your partner. These stressors drain our energy and cause us to feel too tired for sex.

One other factor responsible for dwindling sexual intimacy is satiation, based off the idea that the more we're exposed to a stimulus, the less enticing it becomes. For instance, too much of the same takeout can become monotonous. This is the same way that your partner's body may become less enticing as you get familiar with every inch of it.

Other issues that are responsible for dwindling sexual intimacy are aging and medical issues.

As men age, testosterone levels drop, and this affects sex drive. For women, pregnancy and childbirth change frequency of sex and sexual satisfaction dramatically. For both sexes, chronic illness, physical injury and weight gain may also lead to declining sex.

This said, it is important for you to realize that your relationship isn't going to fail and shouldn't just fall apart because the sexual aspect isn't as hot and powerful as it was many years ago.

This also said, it is important to make a concerted effort to nurture physical intimacy with your spouse. Sex is very important in a relationship and bonds partners together. This is why couples are most likely to report a lack of sex when they feel that they are drifting or growing apart. Overall bonding and sexual intimacy are closely connected.

Sex is vital to the degree that it makes a couple happy, and the quality and frequency of sex that makes a couple happy will vary from couple to couple and will depend on factors such as their ages, values, innate sex drive, lifestyle, health, and the quality of the relationship.

So how do you get your sex life out of the rut? This is where maintenance sex comes in.

Simply defined, maintenance sex is basically "I am not really in the mood but let's get it on anyway," sex. This may be or may not be planned in advance.

There are three reasons that maintenance sex is essential to the success of long-term relationships.

First, the biggest problem that most couples is the problem getting in the mood. Couples often explain that although they were initially reluctant, they had a great experience nevertheless once they made the plunge to have sex. For most of us with busy lives, it is the 'getting started' that constitutes the problem.

Secondly, there is hardly any couple that is perfectly synced in their sex drives. There are instances where one person wants sex more often than the other, and there are instances where one may want it when the other doesn't. It is important to understand that this variation is completely normal. This is why indulging one partner in a romp when the other isn't initially in the mood can be good for the relationship, as long as both parties are wholly on board.

Thirdly, couples need psychological and verbal intimacy before they can attain sexual intimacy. Maintenance sex might in this respect be healthy because it makes you talk about your needs and desires both outside and inside of the bedroom.

Let's not forget that how frequently a couple should have sex is dependent on their peculiar relationship. You and your partner should openly discuss what feels healthy for you, and then create some downtime in a way that meets each other's needs. It probably will not feel sexy at first, but as you go on, this will foster bonding and emotional intimacy and help to improve sex drive and passion.

To further ignite your sex drive and satisfaction with your partner, here are some other things you can do:

- Introduce new stimuli and spice things up. Don't get stuck in the same position and style forever, Try out new sexual positions, new toys, lingerie, games and fantasies.

- Keep technology out of your bedroom. This means removing the TV from your room, and an actual alarm clock instead of putting your cell phone on the nightstand as the alarm then reaching out for it first thing in the morning.

- Make sure both of you orgasm. We all know that women statistically have fewer orgasms than men, but both of you should work hard to make sure your partner orgasms. It makes for a better sex drive.

- Build intimacy in your everyday life because overall relationship happiness leads to more fulfilling sex. Get the kids a babysitter and plan date nights. Work on projects together and make the time to connect.

- Identify and reduce the stressors in your life. Stress is an inevitable part of adult life, but you should work to lower the stress in your life, as stress is a major libido killer.

- Get to the root of the matter. When two people who love each other don't have sex at all or regularly, there is a reason and you can use open dialogue to get to the heart of the matter.

DR. MYESHI WILLIAMS-BRILEY

NOTES

CONCLUSION

The message of this book has been very simple. Emotional affairs often start off as harmless friendships but they are incredible deadly to the health of any relationship. In fact, the after effects of emotional affairs are often as disastrous, if not more disastrous than the after effects of a physical affair.

The person who has been cheated on goes through a whole range of emotions upon finding out about the affair, emotions ranging from rage, to sadness, loss of self-esteem or self-confidence, jealousy, shame, emptiness, possessiveness, and annoyance.

It does not however mean that a relationship that has gone through the horrors of cheating is doomed. Despite the heartache that follows upon discovery, there is still hope that this relationship can be salvaged, that it can be redeemed into a whole new and wholesome relationship. The salvaging of such a relationship however requires the cheater to be repentant, the victim to be forgiving, and the two of them willing to put in the work required to rebuild their relationship.

This is the whole message of the book, and I pray with the fullness of my heart that you have been able to read, understand and receive this message. Beyond that, I pray that the truths you have learned here will help you restore your marriage and have a stronger relationship going forward.

And I pray with the wholeness of my being that you never ever go through the heartbreak of an affair again.

Love,

Dr. Briley

How to Contact Dr. Myeshi Williams-Briley
P.O. Box #2953 Spring TX 77383-2953
Follow her on YouTube

About the Author...

Dr. Briley is the proud CEO/Founder of ESHI Therapy Center which is Education, Support, Help and Intervention Center (owned and operated by her for 26 years). At the center, many are helped through intervention/counseling support. She has a diverse dynamic background of the many things she has accomplished in her life.

She was the President/CEO of the Spring-Klein Chamber of Commerce for 5 years. Community Liaison for the City of Houston's Coast2Coast Rx Card program, in 2019 she also purchased a new business called Blue Scorpion Property Preservation Management Group. In 2017 she launched a new project called Texas Pearl Girl 66, which is an online Pearl Store, that gives back a certain amount to help stop Texas Human Trafficking. Dr. Briley has more than 26 years of Philanthropist work done around the word and community/business experience.

She is a volunteer speaker concerning epilepsy/neurological disorders issues, severed as a board member of A Heart Like Hers Foundation and a past member of the Barbara Jordan Ambassador Program Health Communication and Media Partnership. She formerly was the health and wellness coordinator at Fallbrook Church and a former charter board member of the Rotary Club of Northwest Houston Sunset. Dr. Briley was an instructor at Prairie View A&M University in the field of Human Services in the Continuing Education Department and was a Part-Time instructor at Belhaven University which is a Christian base University. She

DR. MYESHI WILLIAMS-BRILEY

currently teaches at Eastern Gateway Community College. Prior to and throughout her community service, she held several positions at a Fortune 500 banking institution for 14 years with a final position as National Operations Risk Manager/AVP Officer.

Dr. Briley received a master's degree in Human Services Concentration in Organizational Management and Leadership from Springfield College. She holds her Doctoral degree from CICA International University in Theological Seminary Studies. She also holds a Honorary Doctorate of Humane Letters from CICA- International University. She holds a Business Retention & Expansion Coordinator Certification, with her business knowledge on how to grow Rural Communities. Dr. Briley also holds many other degrees in service and business. She was appointed to the Texas Special Education Continuing Advisory Committee in 2011 to 2013 by Governor Rick Perry. In 2013 she was reappointed to the committee to serve Texas again and completed service in 2017. In 2012 Dr. Briley also served and was appointed by the governor to the State Supervision Board for the State of Texas to 2017. In 2014 to 2015 she was appointed by Governor Rick Perry to serve Texas Manufactured Housing Board. She has received numerous awards for philanthropist work in the community/business involvement around the word. In 2012 Dr. Briley, was nominated for the Texas Women Hall of Fame through the Governor's office of Rick Perry for her works around the world. She has helped provided schools in South Africa with books and resources to learn. In 2016 she was asked to be on the Klein ISD Career and Technical Education Advisory Council to help in keeping the CTE curriculum relevant to business/industry needs and ensure Klein ISD graduates are capable of successfully of entering the world of work and post post-secondary education. In 2017 she was asked to be on the Boy Scouts of America Iron Horse District Community, where they find local fund support in the community to help support the mission and vision of Boy Scouts of America for Spring TX. She currently serves on Memorial Hermann (The Woodlands TX Medical Center Advisory Council) and Harris SA Texas Children HP Star Kids Member Advisory group. In 2015 Dr. Briley, was labeled Influential Women in business. Dr. Briley has written many articles on works in philanthropist world and business / self-improvement and family/relationships. She is a true philanthropist of today's time. She is also the President/CEO of 1Voice 1Blanket Foundation. The City of Houston has given Dr. Briley her own day for the successful work of philanthropy that she has accomplished in Houston and around the world. The day is on January 1, given to Dr. Briley by Annise D Parker former Mayor of The City of Houston in 2013.

One of Dr. Briley dreams would be to one day get the Key to The Great City of Houston for all the work she has done and continue to do.